Red Head
A Reparation for Cruelty

Poems of the Unknown Soldier

Red Head

by
AE Reiff

Austin, Dallas, Phoenix
Newfoundland Books
2022

CONTENTS

Acknowledgments

I was walking the shores of Snowdonia where lines of old battle poems were whispering. In the resignation of the fallen who cultivated an agriculture of the praises of Jesus. Composed in ballad-like forms bards might sing to welcome the King of Kings and Lord of Lords of hearts, flowers, plants and stars, as a river washes over stones in the clay, Red Head continues the embassy of that chapbook, The True Light That Lights (2020). Celebrated here in the Lake Country, Stonehenge, Glastonbury, the Tor, Old Sarum and Bath, the first lines of the lyric of that unknown soldier began in Red Head as a villanelle, "Only three have returned from the battle's rage," were begun while driving late one night. The impressions of dozens of sites in Anglesey and Caernarvonshire of the agony of war, the worship of God, the love of woman continued as "I held this image in my mind of red on gold." Some of these poems of the true subject of every country and person presume Aneirin at the battle of the Gododdin at Catraeth. Many of the poems in this collection appeared in *The Texas Quarterly, Lucille 3, Latitude 30 18', Awhile, Ygdrasil: A Journal of the Poetic Arts, G. Dance's Penny's Poetry Blog, Ink Pantry, Emanations 9, Frigg, The True Light That Lights, Recon and The Sparrow's Trombone* to whose entities grateful acknowledgment is made.

For Magister in Artibus
(Prifysgol Cymru Bangor)

THE UNKNOWN SOLDIER

BARLEY FEED

There is a harvest in a cutting down,
In the shed blood of the speared hero,
There is a redding of the land
Before green graves under sod.

Gold the heroes of valor, gold,
Directed to heaven, not strangers,
Wise men, they leave a country,
Dropping like fruit from a tree.

I am rich in cultivation,
A soft plough, I rend the ground,
The grasses, the aired bodies,
Stir about the break of day.

No sparing of the vine nor branches,
So outstretched the whitened lances.
An ardent star across the lightening field
No trembling saw that lofty hill concealed.

First flowers on these mountains
My wealth, the treasured sun,
The purpled blades shed blood.
No piercéd then would not be pierced again.

Now earth, be made sweet by this barley feed.

RED HEAD

Alone by bloom from the root
Or in beds from seed begun,
There is a crimson head
In the spring-brightened loam.

Here's a bloom that died
Alone in the sunlit plain,
But it will not return alone
When sun warms earth again.

They feel the fallen spring rain
Who the ground concealed,
Twice-new, the air they regain,
Death only increases their yield.

The blood of the wounds of the world
Thus the red flower shed,
"I lay on the bloody field,
I it was who bled."

FIELD

Long the days and long the nights
I held this image in my mind of red on gold,
Blood on flowers, bold furrows
sweep the valley to a glade.

It is a glade I know, but thunders one hill
That rests a back into ground so still.
Three hundred had fallen of bright Gwynedd's horde,
Bright battalions with their blue bright swords.

Bright battalions with their blue bright swords!
On the strand white lances, clear mead was the sea!
Flames of shedding blood, steel blades by heaps of dead,
Already ravens were croaking above blood.

SONG

Only three have returned from the battle's rage
(Ab Edmund, Siôn Eos are gone)
And I who was bleeding to sing this song.

Now these had been given a second day
To die, for the battle was long.
Only three have remained from the battle's rage

Where they lingered until the bright dawn.
There I strolled arm and arms in the glade,
And I, who was bleeding, to sing this song

even more for the battle my pay,
as I bend and shake like the corn.
Only three have returned from the battle's rage

I saw Edmund and Siôn in the sun,
Our heroes were gone about break of day,
And I, who was bleeding, to sing this song

Come at last no more from my grave,
I, Edmund, Siôn Eos are one.
Only three had returned from the battle's rage
And I, who was bleeding, to sing this song.

GREEN HILLS

September is the cruelest month,
It brings new worlds of war,
At noon its surface bore our boats
where the green hills come to shore
From the everlasting ways
of peace and war.
The hills
reflect our feet, the evening hills
of sunlit face reflect
what the winds repeat
of the everlasting ways.

THE PLANT

I live among you though you know me not,
But knowledge came to me found out of doubt,
Hear, see me on my stem, I have come out,
For now I rise and bloom while you're about.
I could but now receive you for I grow
Nearer to where my Lord his veins let flow,
He has me and he will not let me go.
I am undone yet he shall be my Lord,
He has into my life his water poured
That I bleed with him for he loves the world.
He loves the world with his own shed blood,
He has given me the way that I should go,
He has taken away all of my will and He would
That I scatter these seeds he would sow.

AMARANTH

Immortal Amarant, a Flower which once
In Paradise, fast by the Tree of Life
Began to bloom, but soon for man's offence
To Heav'n removed where first it grew, there grows,
And flowers aloft shading the Fount of Life.
And where the river of Bliss through midst of Heaven
Rolls o're Elysian Flowers her Amber stream;
With these that never fade the Spirits elect
Bind their resplendent locks enwreathed with beams.
Paradise Lost, III: 353-361.

Where Love-Lies-Bleeding stretches all bejeweled,
I watch the fields that purple with their blood,
Incarnate flowers quicker turn to red,
A spark, a torch, forgotten in a flood.
Was this their care and that a sign, to light
The mine of spice that fills the heart? Or must
The crimson drape of time obscure the flight
Of sunlight fleeing from the mind of dust?
There flowers bloom a vein of Love and Life
To wind about a disembodied cross,
But lose into the earthly air their life,
As night, dark sun, burns darkly on their loss.
And now my heart is but an aging sack,
For Love's gone to the world and won't come back.

From their blissful Bowers
Of Amarantin Shade, Fountain or Spring,
By the waters of Life, where ere they sat
In fellowships of joy: the Sons of Light
Hasted.
Paradise Lost, XI: 77-81f.

REPARATION

"O never could be found Garments too good
For Thee to wear, but these, of thine own blood."
Richard Crashaw

We take the blessing that our Lord has given,
The life that fills our hearts here under heaven,
Releasing all our care into that sea
Where by reflection we resemble Thee,
Our Lord-Who-Marked-The-Heaven,
so we trust, whatever marred him, it was
God bruised him, no other beauty we desire thus
Who join with him, no form nor comeliness.

Carry your sorrow, bear your grief to one
pierced breast of love, the Lord's,
and there we lie, but for his pain and our iniquity,
Save for another One would dare to die.
He died with us while we were yet in sin
And here our peace and victory begin.

SACRED HEART

Oh Lord before, I knew thee for my food,
The only nourishment on which to dine,
My promised former love I now renew,
For worldly fortune I have all resigned
The flesh I seek to give already thine.
A feeding rose has given me this sign
Of nourishment, its root within the ground,
There flows the spring of springs and my buds swell,
His image I embody where I dwell
When I abide within the Lord I've found.
He at the wedding feast who would elect,
Who says to me my friend accept my peace
And purity to heal and come accept
My heart and living on my love so feed.

ELEGY
For Henry Burlage

You came like love, a day, you leave the same,
The sad week, now the month, the year will bring,
You rose before the dawn, though might have stayed,
When you, who past resolved your life, took wing.

In a man's last days a stillness comes,
And though he speak of other times and more,
He'll "live to ninety," as his race is run,
The periods of stillness then grow more and more.

Out before dawn, all day among the doves,
You sing barefoot and lazed with earth again,
As all men live they end their days on love,
And suddenly last promises from you they win.

THE BODY

"The spiritual did not come first
but the natural, and after that the spiritual."

I lay in bed trying to get my breath,
slept a long hour or two before dawn,
gradually I became aware my body
had risen slightly from its sleeping form.
This felt good so I didn't move,
went in and out of sleep several times.
I could hear differently then,
wheezing groans, coughs and forced breaths
and sounds like long sonorous moans.
I was either asleep in this raised state
hearing my own flesh cry out in pain,
or awake hearing the world's sound,
loud early in night which had since calmed down.
It was like a train or a moan the world cried out,
a patient deep in pain this resonant thing
with a mellow groan and travail.
I heard it snoring in some detail.
I conclude from this a spiritual world exists,
that its spiritual body lacks sense
and that something is terribly wrong
if it makes these sounds like an old folks home.
Back in flesh I didn't hear it again.

BROTHER'S SONG

"Come about in time again," Egypt enchoired,
Echoing like an inner triangle,
"Come down the Nile again, be desired,
O come down again!"

Space ahead and away, Israel shone
In the Light of Lights,
"Come round to Jerusalem,
He has desired to come again."

Round again. Christ expired between
Like a spray of rose enfolding the sun,
"Come into your heart and be mine
As love come round again."

THE WAY INTO THE FLOWERING HEART

The way into the flowering heart
Inside the flowering man
Is over the inside itself
Inside the newfoundland.
The head is hot, the hands
Are colder than the air
The arctic-heat will kill away
The spring the petals bear.
The bursting stalk above the eyes
Takes root into the brain
And waves the life of the waving world
Into the heart again.

DITHYRAMBS

When your father grows up
and your mother grows up
and the world grows up
and you grow up,
when you help your neighbor grow up,
and when you love the world,
when you love the life of the world
of blossoms and waves
and the nectar waves
grow way up high
and we see you fly,
do be kind to yourself and neighbor,
do be kind to myself and me,
do be kind to the blooms in blooming
so everybody sees
that when you love the world
you're loving the life of the world
and then you love the world.

PLEASANT THINGS

There is an apple tree with gentle flowers
That grows beside a meadow on a stream,
Its fragrance captivates the wondrous hours
to this one dream, that wandering
Each night I gathered in the heavens,
Violets and the Rose of Sharon and lay
Them beneath the shining blossoms that fall
And thus I labored late into the day.
I came to the orchards by night
And stood in the appled light, the white
Blooms falling to the earth. There gathered
I the meadow sweet I have obtained.

MAY POEM

Will we grow old my dear, our petals wear
Like thin and timeless time-worn lips,
Will this flesh fade even like the rose,
Gone back to its wrinkled root?

All at its full thy flesh I took,
And knew you in wondrous ways now forgot,
The bloom of the breasts, the dew on the skin,
Will these pass like the rest?

Once did we run in fields, raise quick knees,
Embraced in a wood, made elegant a glade,
Even now we embrace and your breath grows hot,
But spring passes and summer will fade.

Time bent with age the gnarled tree,
Increased the girth, made rough the skin,
Think you that this shall fall to you and me
When we're to our bodies again?

VOYAGE

Taliesin came   to storm tossed earth
There in the world   between death and birth
It was his to learn   that he could not save
God it was in the   salt sand wave
If you visit with him   in that good night
You know the earth   will be filled with light

I will be satisfied   when I awake
My deadly wounds   they are not so great
In the lingering goodness of God's heart
He breathes bends bleeds till the heaven parts
The words of God   pure silver words
In them he saw the beauty of the Lord

With angel of the Lord that the saint surrounds
We exalt his name   with the heavenly sound
He delivers the poor   both man and beast
We cease from anger   delight in peace
Living and in death   it is his mirth
To save by sacrifice   and inherit earth

But Taliesin   was not told all
 I met him in the worlds where no night falls
We shared meat and bread sat on a stone
It was that time that   I learned this song
Learned to distinguish   the great and least
And that the Lord loves both man and beast

Once I was young   but now I'm old
Still I wait in the corner of this old sheepfold
I'm a sort of a shepherd catch sheep for the sun
And I wait in the earth till the Lord should come.
Once I thought   the universe fulfilled,
But it was only my heart that he tilled.

PRAISE POEMS

THE BRIGHT EXTENSIVE WILL
For Beatrice

As starry seas are caught up into clouds
To whirl Earth's sphere throughout all time,
Through space and out, where rising in a shroud
They roll the bright extensive will to find
Their will to fall again in showers, so crowds
Descending off the wheel give misty signs
Of life, and sons of Elohim who bow
From out the sky, concentrated and blind
In all their beams, then enter creation.
As though one could with the word written
In earth's center in the matter of its making,
As earth's heart was into pieces breaking,
Come into the body. Then wars should cease,
And earth, all surface, sky and core, find peace.

ANGEL STANDING IN THE SUN

It came about a sun all blazing bright
had showered gold into the heart of man,
as clouds transparent sprung with golden light
like wings of angel's gold through blood then ran.
And shining out in glory still like light
a being light-radiant of golden man,
whose living passion like a redding sun,
with bright and fragrant flames of gold had run.
To you in whom all gold has been perfected,
First Begotten of the fire and flood,
My heart is raised to your sole light protected,
Blaze there thou Daysman in the fiery blood.
My thought is ever sprung from one desire,
That please you to burn sole within this fire.

TO TAME THE KINGDOMS LET HIS ANGELS RUN

Lift up your eyes and look unto the hills,
God's glory is declared from the heaven,
He warms the earth as though the living sun
That causes plants to grow and rivers run
From Him had sprung the meadow and green tree
Lift up a branch and all in praise of Thee.

Man he created sovereign under heaven
To joy him in the light-renewing sun,
There in his veins the dancing rivers run,
But he's as much a mine as he's a tree
That lifts a branch and sings his praise of Thee
Who lit the dawn and raised the blooming hills.

There was an angel standing in the sun
Amid the solar flare where rivers run
Who sang, the heaven's a plant, celestial tree
With garnished fruit that stems its praise of Thee.
When stars are trees, then galaxies are hills,
Where poets dream embodied still of heaven.

All through the night earth's springs and rivers run
While orchards rest in fields, the apple tree
Outgrows from earth between us, me and thee,
And if clouds sink upon the summer hills,
Surround our infancy under the heaven,
Then as we grow clouds part, outshines the sun.

Is it man or heaven, the springing tree
Whose green boughs so transpire their love of thee?
All praise the growth that lies upon the hills.
Stand on your feet you men, look at the heaven,
Redemption near, he comes with light, the son
To tame the kingdoms lets his angels run.

Heaven, earth, man, tree, praise the living God, thee
Who wrought salvation, light and life upon the hills.
Rejoice you lands, he comes, the king of heaven
Whose glory so outshines the lowering sun
That spinning globe that round him ever runs
Will cease and root in his eternal tree.

SON RISING
For Marie

Jesus is in the earth, now springs alive,
He leads the faithful saints into the heaven,
No more shall we within the body strive,
But free of dust and earth shall follow him.
His light shines brighter than the nearest sun,
His light whose volume fills the planes of space,
The whirling stars will slow their rotation,
And galaxies, grown flowers of his grace
Stretch on their stems and open wide their hearts.
There is no more expanse than in his love.
He frees the mighty, lightens darkened hearts
And his own Excellence his glory proves
This is the Lord that I have loved from birth.
He comes to rule and thus to save the earth.

THE BRANCH

When
the Lord of All
descended into flesh,
came through the
million worlds
into the one
of mercy,
wisdom,
beauty,
love,
unlike the prism that divides the ray,
undiffused, he came into the body's clay,
the Son
of the
Divine
Wisdom,
the Son, the
Incarnate
Redeemer.
Our world
has been
recovered
by his being
no extra-
terrestrial
intelligence;
his human body
shaped it to a tree
that roots in wisdom
but whose beauty's trunk
to the earth sphere a branch extended,
on that tree the Lord Beauteous hung suspended,
and then we were enabled to receive him.

CHRISTMAS TREE

Now is Christ my Christmas tree,
evergreen not dry,
his roots grow into his own stream
and into him flow I.

Blessed are the waters that freshly flow
From his incarnate stream,
Transpire in the living bough,
Fall in the rain.

I came to the water and thirsted,
sought for his Lamb light,
that God given Tree of Life,
I bought his water right.

Who has not seen his limbs outstretched,
boughs with his blessing,
beauty and grace bowed down to us,
fragrant pressing.

Now is he my Christmas tree,
my ornament of life,
his roots grow into his own stream
and into him flow I.

A GREEN TREE

There is no cold in Christ nor winter storm
To chill the bone, there is no frost in him,
No freeze there kills the stem, no ice brings harm.

He lives in us to keep his branches warm,
A green tree ever rooted deep within,
There is no cold in Christ nor winter storm.

There where the harvest hills through summer run
To fall, he keeps a barn, a winter bin,
No freeze there kills the stem, no ice brings harm.

He has into us all his flowers sown
A seeding of himself, garden within,
There is no cold in Christ nor winter storm.

He there a gardener of his lovely plants, forms
Protoplasm and a living mind,
No freeze then kills the stem, no ice brings harm.

The Rose of Nazareth, Lord to flesh was born,
Accept his seed sons, daughters, women, men,
There is no cold in Christ nor winter storm,
No freeze there kills the stem, no ice brings harm.

RIVER ROCK
For Darryl King

The water of this river fed by springs
has overrun the stones hid in the clay.
The flood erodes the lively stones,
reveals surface, depth, in large and small,
This took ten thousand seasons of the leaf in all.

Whatever was the reason, kindred souls
who lived and died took earth.
They lived for the purpose of its restoration.
Just as the flood revealed the stones in clay,
These assembled at the latter day.

There where the river ran over us we lived
and learned to build the one, the spiritual friend.
Christ ran over us, some to lift and blend,
Some peacefully rested he in banks here under sand.
But now the flood bares open the whole bed of the stream
And the righteous are revealed, or so we learn.

ON A CONJUNCTION OF PLANETS
for Robert and Cynthia

What lover's open lips we are tonight
In time the endless world, our minds unfurled
Into and out of each other, the light-
Cast summer sky, the light-borne orient world
With planets never seen appears to be,
The lady Venus, she Hesperide,
Is open in the moon's new horn who now
Is casting all her smile by the sun
And as red mars rings to a russet core
There too is Saturn hid within a mist
Of rings eternal, smiling all the more
As if the four that rolled together kissed.
And while this change is happening in the sky
We marry all our loves in Gemini.

PATTERN

If I a pattern of the universe divine,
Stars and plants see joined in luminous light,
Hear the wind's song, thunder in heart and mind,
That these portend symbols of universal might,
Then I consider first their means of union,
The balance of beauty with power and force,
What adherence! God seems like a woman,
Holds together his family of atoms from wars.
Out far within deep the reach of dark space,
He acts on this pattern of union for earth,
When he marries, he is husband and spouse,
Birth his great mystery, creation of life,
So while he acts as our father and mother,
all along we knew him as our lover.

HEAVEN'S MAN

Who then first found the cosmos in a man,
Divided minutes of his arc, set axis?
If man be heavens, then heaven is for man,
And this his truth, how big the universe.
He is no sun that planets orb and orb,
Or like the moon, his body old and dead,
Nor is he earth, that planet swirling through
His sphere, or other, Mars or Jupiter.
What is man that heaven admired him,
Or sons of men to be so greeting them?
Creating heaven with a touch, his fingers,
God gave to man dominion of his hands.
In all the world and worlds beyond oh Lord,
I seek to serve you and to know your word.

SPOUSE

I hold you now when once I did but seek
to know unrisen, the one Daystar,
I sensed your coming then but I was weak,
and also at that time I was at war.
It was not simply felt this destiny,
A door where inward certitude of sense
like dawning light from dark I felt give way.
I could but ask the sun to run its course,
but now the way's so clear that can distract
my seeing mind from its first choice and heart.
In all these acts the outer mode is less
clear now we're joined than when apart.
What of it though, now that I hold you close?
It's only my confusion I have lost.

I WISDOM

"The Lord brought me forth as the first of his works, before his deeds of old…before the mountains were settled in place, before the hills, I was given birth…I was there when he set the heavens in place," (Proverbs 8, 22-31)

There was an angel in the height
Who took a long roll, then clouds
Were lifted. Under my wing was the light
Of the presence within
Eternal life.

I floated to the third dimension
In a cube of yellow hair.
With the eternal somersaults of light
I caught apple blossoms as they fell to earth,
They were so fair.

A point in the line of stellar trajectories,
I was Mars when you landed me,
Solar fire when you felt me,
I was on the outermost planet
Astride the gloom.

I was historical persons,
Signed the Declaration.
I was the centurion who loved his servant.
I fought underground
Where I died.

I rose in mist from a stream in the morning,
I surrounded the fragrance of new mown hay,
I was shaping clouds for evening,
Choosing colors, the first rose, the purple
End of the day.

I was a last leaf in fall
Until I was alive in the redbud tree.
I nested all winter with waxwings.
Joined early robins in wet hills
Under cedar.

Who do you think I am while you are reading?
When the word takes inspired flame I ignite.
I am the word in all of its meanings,
Put into sentences I leap up, oh wisdom,
I incarnate.

Where will I be when you are seeking me?
Shall I stand upon the ground and smile invisibly?
Will you think to look for me in a bad man?
Will you think I am in your heart,
Inconsolable?

I was the question of a trusting child,
I fought back an answering reply,
I was the disillusioned, the rejected heart,
Though I yearned, this also I did not embrace.
I wept.

I ripened the fig on its branch, turned a pear
Green to gold. I was polishing apples
With my long reach. Filling the fertile seed
With two weeks' growth, I prepared the ground
For my harvest.

Am I so selfish in my cOre for the living?
I rode the seed in the belly of a bird,
Was cast out, this lime made me fertile,
I spread in groves, a dozen at once, solitary
In vacant fields.

I cared for the man whose ashes were scattered,
Could reproduce him at once from a speck.
I will reassemble the billions, bring them all with me,
I have not forgotten, but my hand is stretched out
To the living.

I wait for the moment when you are alone,
When all the seeds of my experience have grown.
I am around you, under you and above you,
Now is the moment to take me at last
To your heart's home.

I crept with luminous fire up trunks and branches,
As the moon rose I set forth with the owl,
Crested tall grasses, hunted
Till the mouse froze, dove with talons,
But not for food.

I was the living stone, from my pores water came.
My body rested back in the hill,
I set the flowing cup upon my table.
I am also a quarry, men come to set me
In their foundations.

I am water, the Wood, the tree,
The rock, the mortar and the building stone,
I make myself of myself myself,
I am in hands, brains, plans, trades,
Who is like me?

I rise in realization of my own being,
Take root in the spreading ground that I filled,
I am awake, synapse of one idea,
Palpable, real, breathe awhile in joy,
My discovery.

While they search for me they know me not,
I come to my own if they will have me,
It is a little thing, I make a man hungry
And I am his bread, thirst and he drinks me,
Filled to the brim.

I tire not easily when I shake the mountains,
I appeared at noon time myself transparent,
I cast no shadow when I took on flesh.
What are these wounds in my hands? If they ask me
I tell them.

I was inspiration for a thousand works,
I held the chisel, I taught the eye,
I was discovery in night, in the day
I remembered myself, let the notes play
From an ink pen.

I am the blind poet, sent to justify
The ways of God to men. I was in the garden,
Before the flood, I was alive
And I live forevermore and
I come quickly.

I was reading a poem, I was the sound
And the voice of the speaker, I sent
For ears, for hearts to fill, I took
The ringing of bells, set verse,
Then I was glad.

I was glad when the core of light opened
And I saw myself coming for my own,
I wore the white robe of day in its dawning,
The sun was an ethereal circle when I stopped
The earth's turning.

Do you know me as apocalypse,
Here where I once turned worlds to improve them?
So you have me alpha and omega, so extreme
For one who turns a plane, applies some polish,
Adjusts a spin.

I was an inherited son, traveled the fir country,
Whence I came when my time was fulfilled.
No different from the foal to its mother, I came
For milk and was feasted, I was loved thus
By my own.

I was still in the vineyard, grown with the grape
In the foot of the vintage, pruned with the vine,
I was harvested in wheat heads, sown in the field,
But even as the feasting began I was
Time's fruition.

I was ages growing, root grew, bud opened,
Have flowered in the century of history,
The stone, wood, spring, well,
Vine and stalk of my being
Just incomplete.

I need a loan from the hearer, must hear the sound
Of hands clapping, this bright adoration,
Hold first blessing over heads made abundant,
Harvest bins fill bursting, thus consumed,
And this by singing.

SOLITUDE SURROUNDED

Speaking
Of the white ace
Of spades in the universe surrounded,
using words like mystic and visionary
to confound each other,
we go our way de-verbalizing verse.
But there is a human need of singing,
of praise to prove us grateful for our being
beyond what the cathode and the radio say,
everyone tells us we're not meant for that.
Different temperaments for all, humanly speaking,
till no one is left in the world but ourselves singing
the Great Solitude, surrounded by the air our gravities attract,
not thoughts like our own but their opposites,
solitude surrounded, compassed by pets,
homes, wives, children, oceans, walls,
When a monastery would have suited best
And
We
Live
Long
Lives.

THE PLANETARY BULLDOZERS ARE COMING

The planetary bulldozers are coming.
Earth mover's novae sound the air,
and soot like the ashes of rain,
ceaseless, untiring.

The planetary bulldozers are driving
witless machines
into unconscious beds of streams,
where antediluvian soils
will be overturned.
They are coming.
Jet engines replace the ocean roar.

Oh what a fruit is the earth
to be peeled and spat,
each element divided
with a mad cat
on its trail.

These are no nightmares.
These no visions.
The moon will beat down
without an eclipse.
The sun will roll its tongue for water.
Adam sees in the mirror nothing at all.
The time is 2000 and more,
Hear the machines roar.

The planetary bulldozers
have come to poor earth.
What will you do when the tow truck stops at your door?

THE BANQUET OF GOD

First in the soles of feet, up into legs and groins,
The crux that leaps, forbidden flower employed
Enflames a sleep. Throw out those books,
Torn papers encrust stone, one walking looks
To where a page of poems brood
Outlined by, ah, the underlined, bright rood.

Home roadway, airport railway, factory,
We eat our fill in earth's refectory.
We have a sewage problem Amazon,
Piped to our cities. We long for you
River of the world to eat our fill,
If you can contain the products of our will.

There is a problem, surely it has been a problem.
One lay across the thwart, the heart, the bleeding stem,
Bled, burned. The boat? The bellowing ash of earth.
There walked children whose eyes gave mirth
To masses who saw their death and died,
So look upon the faces with unaverted eyes.

The grass caught fire, leapt trees, on fire his hair,
On fire the man you will see running there.
He leapt into a pool of sparks, redux,
burning coals became a barbecue.
All cows were happily so consumed, goats lept
Upon grills, sheep tendered their loins and slept.

Burn heavens, light mountains now you candles,
Drain rivers, seas drain, or were you vandalized?
Awake cave dwellers, for once upon a time
in meadow, grove and stream you unapparelled find
in celestial light, the forest wrong,
At first the groves but then the trees are gone.

And the song, of outlandish devils shame,
Imbedded from the mast of earth, who blames?
The flavor is an appetizing boil,
Charcoaled, grilled to ash, unspoiled.
Our meat was in the fire cooking
Consumed throughout. How's that looking?

Pigs, chickens gave them up to farce,
Alone among foods, vegetables last dished.
There is a hunger now, would you be warned?
There is a thirst, you should not go unarmed.
So the world turns, the daily sight
Continues its delight.

Silence pipettes in radioactive milk,
Nonsense takes a mercury sandwich, silt,
But no DDT. Don't spare the topsoil,
Stung before dismembering. No microbes toil.
No sky will fall nor mountain cease to clap
When hands, though terrors, possess not this abstract.

Here proclaim a time when meadow, grove and stream
Were filled, backfilled, trucked off. What does it mean?
Authorized, certified, entirely official,
Back to nature we got an administrative bushel.
There man can better himself
If not by worth he takes the earth by stealth.

Good funding institutes these bonds
Where Procter and Gamble compose a split gene round.
Pyruvate phosphatase* the daily song repeats,
Science and business sing. No defeat For cruelty.
The knowing herd, the drifting dark
Comes to noon, sun shines, burns heart.

Tear turf, rip ravines, ruined cities judge first
yourself. This is the way that God is just.
When business empires whiten without,
There within clerks and executives, doubt
Inks margins to encroach the light,
Which sport enables the approaching eon night.

Look, this is hell and there the savior walks
Among coals, pitted ruins, idle talk.
There it was among industrialists
He leaned into rubbish, proved to exist
This token of hope against war, to tell
How first with angel fire the first trump fell.

Still it's a bit ticklish, the feeling
When the hair falls out as the skin is peeling.
Admit it. Trees never had leaves.
The telling those old wives' tales must cease.
Come over for the visit, the erosions' not too bad,
It's not the flash, it's the light and shock that's sad.

We lost a third part of the atmosphere.
Nothing was spared. There was a sale at Sears.
The innocent working bee, bacterial spring,
The inward warmth, tree rings,
The cynic died a horrid death,
We saw him as he was, unstaunched and luminous.

Lover's bone to sinew broken, ligaments
Peacefully expired, the hair fell into place.
You mistake. Ignorance feels nothing.
What returns? Iniquity, cowardice, slumping.
Why think a heart of beef, calves' liver
Less human than this pumping gesture?

When I cut the heart into usable pieces,
I mean when I sought experimental protein
For the lab of judgment there was no meat
At all, fatty substance unusable, sweet,
Outpoured ill got sentiment,
I never knew just what it meant.

Rain fire clouds, smoke heartily ravines
Lift continents angelic gravities.
Juggle its pieces into air, Time's filled,
there is no way the earth were spared.
We shall not say it was the fault of man.
No man indeed. Indeed it was no man.

Come all to this great supper, press wine,
And heavenly birds you also come to dine.
One Pompeii blast or Ceres' quake will bend
The fine earth, shake, lift sea and hems.
There is another sphere, come worms and flies,
Raveners to great sacrifice.

From pits come vultures, eagles come to fish,
The lambs must wait now man is the dish.
Earth cleansed, war with him has gone,
Come beasts, coyotes, dogs and learn to carnivore.
Come bear, panther, bobcat find your spouse
And breed, the earth's your wedding house.

Progeny extinct, come poison fish.
Mercury snakes from inert wood.
Calculate the final layer of mud
Where even the bacteria find no food.
This witness from the art invite
But banquet first, this food is ripe.

When once at the predicted end of time
Forgiven my sins and rhyme

Certified, I came to the wedding,
Rose in the mist, spread across a flooded plain,
It seemed the ghost of all the souls who died
Mammalian successors and antecedents sighed.

Come to the palpable spirit wreck
ghosts swarmed air like soundless bees to seek
The million million stings themselves,
It was no cries with which the air was filled.
Air smokes and solid forms melt.
Was there a sun? Not that my senses felt.

Stone ran a common river, molten steel
a monument when it congealed. The night air cooled,
there was an evening breeze,
O attic shape, what pipes and timbrels these?
Who comes to sacrifice? What have they forged?
Thus my earth hungered even while it gorged.

NIGHTINGALE

I.

Prince Edmund sang in metered rhyme to these
Nine lines tuned from Italian romance,
Now I begin the numbers thus to please
The mind and occupy the sense:
If Shelley, Byron, Keats could take the chance
To try to muster time to his desire,
So now a living wight will join their dance;
See how the dark that was once so dire,
May yet revive and kindle new a sea of fire.

II.

And seas of fire even yet we'll know,
As Beowulf stands beside the burning mere
Of plumb immensity before he'll go
Into the vast abysm without fear,
And wonders if that watery bed's his bier
Before he draws a breath of earth's sweet air
And dives into the darkness of the mere:
Just so I reckon it's not comfort's lair,
Unless it be to seek a grand adventure there.

III.

So as the numbers fall from one to ten,
To climax twelve within a single line,
And then my bubbles surface to you friend,
Think nothing less than nothing if you find,
That nothing's gained when nothing has been rhymed:
As sunlight on the shining sea is seen
In glints and glimmers, each a different kind,
So like diffracted light must now I seem
A wretch that seeks to hold a beauty that's unseen.

IV.

Fair, loving beauty, how within the dark
You seem like Grendel's dam behind the mask
Of waters I approach to hellish barks.
Is it the hound or hounds of hell whose task
Was lately muzzled and their jaws held fast
By Heracles? The heroes go before,
And at the end of time who follows last
Of all to the already closing door
Will hear the whispering waters then become a roar.

V.

Enough lament, now turn we to the theme,
Whose gentle guide the gentle only bear,
For she will rage and yet she's beauty's queen,
Who though unknown and black is yet so fair
That you will give your very life to dare
The deepest mire, lacking but yourself,
And leave the labor of this life's poor care,
To reach the glory of her wondrous wealth:
Nor will I wait to go for honor, fame or health.

VI.

Her name is Nightingale whose story's known
To start while she was gazing at a stream,
Where sudden from within his stygian home
She by the murky Dis at first was seen,
To be so fair, so fit for ravishing,
For he of late was boasting of his power
Imperious to Love, so that Love deemed
To fire than cranky heart with his soft arrow:
So fired, away Dis flew to pluck this fairest flower.

VII.

I cannot guess what only Dis may know,
He may be though most blind from what he's caught,
But he could learn from Merlin in the stone,
Who in unguarded moment's pose would oft
Then teach to her that which himself was taught,
Might wish him that he never took to wife,
But sought the happy apple boughs aloft,
For now she binds him in the stone: a strife
Forever ceasing so that now begins for life.

VIII.

Fell-fated that moment thus Nightingale
Interred long night, for there the dragon sits,
But she behaved herself, nor would she be
Enamored of his being of the pits,
Oh could she somehow quench his burning fits!
But Dis then with his jenny round her wound
A muslin of his own thick mystic wits,
Her gold and red and green he turned to brown,
Not even now, nor then, has remedy been found.

IX.

Now you who've never been below should know
The trees and grass are black with ageless time,
A kind of moss grows there, no holy wells nor snow,
But many pomegranates grow, they line
The path descendant, but no other sign
Of life is found save that within the fruit:
Then dusky Dis these seeds made into wine,
And calling forth his slave with Orphee's lute,
With this sad song and drink made thus to her his suit.

X.

Forget the ivory dawn my dear, forget
The grain and corn that still the earth must love,
Come take to you a deathless art and let
Us to each other silently so prove
With wordlessness, no witness tell, nor move
To any tales how our hearts knit, nor give
Account of what we do, nor say how wove
This fabric of our garment. Unquestioned
Thus our love will die, so it must dying live.

XI.

Much like a transformed beast the winded Dis
Then seemed to Nightingale so bright,
Twice lucid were his eyes that promised bliss,
Would she but deign to leave the world of light,
And take the jewel he hung before her sight,
Oh if she'd only known that this his plight
Of troth was remedy of his design,
To keep her in his arms himself throughout all time.

XII.

Of these the arms plutonic poets sing,
When in a verse the beauty that they see,
Like rubies set within a silver ring,
That speak of passion and of ecstasy,
But also pain of our mortality,
They fit with cunning words to their design,
And lift each one to his eternity,
So in the moment's transport of a line,
We change not and forget the ebb and flow of time.

XIII.

So struck and rapt love's heaven in his eyes,
No wit nor thought could pull her from the dream,
Transfixed, her heart could bare hold back its sighs,
Her lips would part and close, and as she seemed
To break, then melt, and forge anew, he deemed
Another time to stop her veiled trance,
For he slacked not: would she then be his Queene?
For like her he unsought had struck Love's chance,
This done they might together wed themselves and dance.

XIV.

Perhaps you think it easy to decide
'Tween life and death, the choice a simple one,
If so this innocent you'll surely chide,
Who yet will sit beside a seely hun,
For she moved not: oh lift your skirts and run,
The chorus sings, seek meadows, the daystar,
Oh choose the lovely beams, the golden sun,
Cast darkness from you lest the world so far
From night your mind forget and be forever barred!

XV.

So might of old Bathsheba counseled be,
When David, King, Beloved by God's own heart,
Royal lion finding her so fair, he
Sought to have the joy and sweetest part
Of this life with the next: the arrow's dart
Took him as he took her, but who could say
Himself so pure than when his own thoughts start
To tend to love, that satisfied today,
Tomorrow would not be where he before did lay?

XVI.

She drank, she drank, who cares to speculate
Argues chiefly of her own volition,
Endeavors she despaired of other state,
Persevers that she thought it was her mission,
Or that she did it from her heart's compassion,
To lose her life, and that without a doubt,
To drink the cup and thus her own perdition,
But in the seed within begin to sprout,
Then in the ripened boughs at harvest time the shout

XVII.

Within her breast in winter sweetly sing:
My root is in the earth, I seek the sun,
I love all growth, the green bud in the spring,
And summer's flower aging have I won,
What in my maidenhood was overcome,
For now I know what my green heart then guessed,
That if I die so then I rise again,
The greater world to bring into the less,
And since my love is ever in the earth: yes, yes.

XVIII.

But the Aegean story intervenes,
For Greek Zeus, the so-called king and god,
Consulting with the powers then decreed
That since our Nightingale would choose to sod
The earth Olympian feet would seldom trod,
She could but half the year her wish fulfill:
The other half, said he, lifting his rod,
She spends with him inside the blooming hill,
And underground his secrets learn whene'er she will.

XIX.

But here is transport to a different clime,
From that on earth wherein we pass our days,
Where loutish verse on earth or hell could shine,
As heaven's pale when covered o'er with haze,
Must, when the wind has changed reveal its maze
Of tunnels, caverns, secret doors and seek
The dark wherein the fragrant unblown waves
Of time are still, familiar world, but bleak,
Eternity compared, beyond compare, makes weak

XX.

The bold who drive their flocks inland from sea:
So with the very vision's rise they fall
Who climb Olympus' height, now so do we,
Into the wondrous night again, and all
Our kind remember what we barely saw,
For colors fade and red goes from the leaf,
This paradox inscribed on heaven's wall:
What has no arms, no legs, no skin, no teeth:
And if you answer it you turn to joy from grief.

XXI.

So as the lonely Dis had her consent,
To fold him in these loving ways, his thirst
Increased to measure hopefulness had meant
To slack, but who can speak of it, the first
Of love is known the best, the last the worst,
Nor did he doubt that in his passion's fire,
The seed of love that Cupid's arrow nursed,
Would of the stygian snake and dark so dire,
Weary of his bed and snakey ways, she'd tire.

XXII.

Come then my fair and only love to guide
My thought return back to its sober theme,
Let us back to hell, where lurks the pride
Of this dark majesty, his loving queen,
The burning lake and Cerberus, who seem
Like phantoms here beside unchanging gods,
But in no change, that's death, if right I deem
My destiny within the heavenly log,
For so also we'll want to know aged Pluto's dog.

XXIII.

Come now sweet Edmund, be my human muse
And balm of thought that gives a verse its high
Epithalamion, for you did choose
To pierce the veil of love and there abide
In piteous looks and groans and softer sighs,
Come now into these lines with gentle taste:
Then sudden did I hear Nightingale cry,
Within the bower see her raptured face,
And then I felt my nerves on fire and my blood race.

XXIV.

Say first the gowns which of themselves let fall
Onto the floor, his all of black with stars
Quick-fired in many hues, that it was all
Light, some burning blue, some red, sapphires,
Lightning winks that children in a jar
Might seek to keep till morning then let loose,
And in gold thread outlined that heavenly car
Of old, once let to Phaethon by Zeus,
That ran the stellar regions then fell from its abuse.

XXV.

Hers was a gown of green and gold that wove
The scenes of pastoral life, of herds and sheep,
Of grain and glade and stream that she did love:
Those rippling fields of gold and whitened wheat
So seemed to move and slowly beat
In measure to soft winds, though lying still,
And in the midst a lady kept her seat,
As from her hair a crown of stars down spilled
Light to a crescent moon whereon her feet were still.

XXVI.

Then in that unlit room there came a light,
Effused in general, near the bed to start,
And opened outward as it seemed my sight
Were changed to some unknown and fragrant part
Of smell: it was the music of their art,
And all seemed turned to rose, oh shade of love,
For then I felt it enter at my heart,
As if it overflowing then must prove
A vast and fired boundlessness to make me love.

XXVII.

Not like a gold or flaming light it came,
But in the soft effulgence lovers' wear,
When they, struck in some muse upon the game
That lovers' play, will seem to be thrice fair,
So that they then will glow with colors rare
When by a passing stranger they are seen,
Who thinks that they a robe of light must wear:
Who does not know what such delight will mean
When one from love's embrace by passers-by is seen.

XXVIII.

But though I stood beside the very veil
Wherein they lay, I could not see within,
For it was dark and thus my vision frail,
But then the rosy light that there had been
Became a deepest blue, whose gentle motion
Makes me no longer able to describe
What seems profane compared to their devotion,
So then to everything my sense there died,
And I into those gentle waves myself did glide.

XXIX.

Nor are these marvels all that we can tell,
For still the chamber must we yet describe,
With walls of porphyry translucent, Hell
Had no likeness to it, for on its sides
Reflected were strange writings so inscribed
That backwards could be read what ne'er is fit
For human eye to read, and we'll not try
To fathom more, lest we untimely trip
Our lives from earth and fall to darkness in our wit.

XXX.

But fate demands that vision prophesy
What already ancient poets had known,
Nor would for Dis dare any justify
That joy, the Nightingale, should leave his home,
That she into the springing plants would grow,
While he alone, translucent by himself,
Would blast with mellow sigh and endless groan,
So that it ever tried the darkest health,
When into bright sunlight and life she took his wealth.

XXXI.

Then did I see him pine about his desk,
For there of old, this loneliness his curse,
Would he engrave in fire to metal pressed,
As if he thought to fill her heart with verse,
Renewing themes upon the wedding hearse,
So to bemuse his late and favored wife,
Who may have thought that her fair heart would burst,
For men will turn with each sweet shaking sight,
But still he loved and unto her these words would write:

XXXII.

My dear, almost alone I spend the night
With thoughts of you, but they are more than thoughts,
In my imagination is the sight
Of your soft eyes o'erlaid in azure, wrought
With gold which in my heart I lock, as fraught
With gold and precious ore below, whose veins
Of light may winter in a star, but not
Above, which others sleep I watch the lane,
And wait until the long days, weeks and months will wane.

XXXIII.

When I'm asleep then you're awake, thus cold
Time conforms us all, for it and space
Conspire against us and so more bold
I conjure you on earth a faster race
Around yourself, that I may soon your face
Of love and more to warm your lips and breasts,
Draw honey from your heart, whose last embrace
I ne'er forget as we inside love's nest
Did linger and draw out of time to very fete.

XXXIV.

Put on the royal robes I once gave you
When on that new moon night our minds first met,
There is the likeness to compare the hue
Of your rare beauty, thought that you set
In fiery letters, though the lips were wet,
And told in silence simple things you heard
Inside my brain: for when all words were let
Alone, most still your thought was clear, no word
Related, only thought as then your thought I heard

XXXV.

So thus I number, use up, another day
Until, regained again, those precious bowers
That in you lie; this dalliance of praise
Will speed the shortened seasons' powers,
For as I sing away will while the hours:
And see your image cast within my breast
Of roses, ivy, amaranth and flowers,
For there we soon will hope to find a rest
When into flowers, buds and stems myself I press.

XXXVI.

Whoever would awake from this sweet bliss,
Sure cannot say, there isn't time to tell
How long it lasts, so long as lovers kiss
I guess, but in the dark I heard a bell,
And thought that of the strange new sights of hell
I'd miss not one, so roused went out to see,
And when I left those yet within were well,
For they were rapt in love nor would miss me
As out into the passageway I passed quickly.

XXXVII.

As ghastly meditations strike the mind
Of those who've died, when silent in the tomb
They from the ways of life themselves unwind,
For then they enter in a greater womb,
Where deities of light cause them to swoon,
The peaceful and the wrathful ghosts to see,
All images they feared while in earth's room,
So now within the dark such thing fright me
As through the narrow tunnels of hell pass quickly.

XXXVIII.

The tinkling bell, the wrinkled dark, the seams
Of darkness sown, as in a critic's eye,
Are moats he'd wish to cross, but though he lean
Into himself will find no boat, so I
Give him free passage in a breaking rhyme.
Take everything and do not leave a bit,
Nor wonder if you better spend your time
In ancient books, there find a better fit,
In dusty works of old a better knit.

XXXIX.

As when in darkness one may see the light,
So down the passageway I went to look,
And wide my arms outstretched to feel what sight
Denied, and if you're bored even with this book,
Then join you in the quest, study forsook
Finds discovery, feel the jagged stone,
So hand in hand with this poor verse a crook
To guide those sheep who think what they must know,
We all with shorn and coldest limbs from life must go.

XXXX.

And these are lines of ordinary men,
Who eat and sleep and love and wake and dream,
Who thus remember one thing out of ten,
And even then in error they may seem
With shades to live, with idle thoughts to teem,
Utopias, Arcadias they would,
For who of better worlds would not oft dream,
And yet we this have not full understood,
For we are men who sought to grasp all that we could.

XXXXI.

Some letters on the darkened walls by torch
I saw, as stumbling over carcasses and bones
I began to pass into the tunnels porch,
And did not think, but still could hear the moans
Of those who tripping, fell upon Hell's stones,
And fallen once they never rose again,
Then did I first begin to feel dark tones,
When I unknowingly into the den
Of Cerberus had gone, the dog that knows not men.

XXXXII.

I recognized, but then it was too late,
The tinkling bell that in a dream I heard,
And feared that bell rang then my mortal fate,
That on its collar rang when that dog stirred,
But then a thought, more like an imaged word
Appeared and spoke, but not out loud, in thought,
There came a growl as if the dog had grrred,
And up it sprang and in its mouth then caught
A turquoise ring which to my trembling hands it brought.

XXXXIII.

What marvel is it that I am not slain,
For then I thought this terror to befriend,
As when Odysseus to spare his pain,
So that against the Cyclops better fend,
Hid in the belly of the sheep to wend
A way to freedom underneath its back,
As now unto this fearsome beast I bend,
Since him from myself I would detach,
And in its belly's fur I placed my hand to scratch.

OLD BARN

Many were the nights I had seen stars,
Each there among the flowers daring smelled
Riches I find only in your arms.
Let me not desire any other
In all these hours, and come beloved,
None many hereafter this know you so well.

And if I may not leave this prison,
Move there like grain in an old barn,
But stored from habitation and old age,
Rooms I keep under the apple tree
Of stone, where I await my love's return,
So to rest in her arms under appley boughs,
In fair a wanton, thus my Queen
Used to hide me in the woodland,
So that when death took everyone
Still it did never call me.

TALIESIN

Now time ends its season
Illustrates the heaven,
Silent the storms of blood,
Eight times the letter proved.
Intent on it he stands,
Listening to his God,
As lost men stop for towns,
Throats clearing, tongues kindling flame.

The bodhisattva twice returned,
Above heaven learned,
Love's sacrifice saves men,
Jesus, creation's Lord, and heaven's.
Every people, lands and men
Shall look on him they pierced,
Irate behold rejected come,
Neighbors and saints judge all earth.

URIEN'S GIFT

Taliessin, bard countenance
All of your fame has not been lost
Long did you serve a king, Urien Rheged
Inside a bag among bull rushes
Elphin the Prince took up this gift
Somber the bards of the isle of Britain
So long without peer in the eye of the west
In praising the God of Creation.
Nine are the letters in the name of Taliessin

Notes

-Taliesin means shining brow.
-Rheged means gift.
-Taliesin was found in a fishing weir.
-Elphin is the son of Rheged.
-The bards are somber because of his excellence.
-Taliesin is a double s in the Welsh.

SONG OF THE WIND

Once like a light in a sculpted city
That now lies dark under fallow ground,
So once the land unknown was full and free,
With cedarn hill and golden meadow found.
I traveled to dawn, went toward the sun
To see this marvelous land, and it was good,
But there I saw a siege works and a gun,
Within the nation tops of watchtowers stood.

I went from the mountains to mourn the nations,
to grieve the fury, destruction and the death,
for over them I saw terror advancing,
fear from the south, destruction from the north
Below there stretched a molten lake,
Which sunset proved to be the blood of men,
It rose to the height of a horse's bridle,
And flowed away with the rain.

I looked in the holy book, inquired
After this fair land, its destiny,
I sought thus many days and nights,
But I had no eyes with which to see.
Wars of Magog, northern powers and lands,
Decrees of pestilence and blood hailstones,
Fire and valleys of bone and I closed the book,
This knowledge was too much for me.

I sat to await the tumult's fall
When I heard a voice of thunder,
And turned to see as if one called from water,
And saw the form of a man.
I was lifted upward from the sun,
There it was, between the earth and heaven,
I saw all things were written in a book,
Which I read not for they are soon to come.

Then one said, these people   need a warning,
Son of man   how shall they hear?
I cried for grace   but his eyes were fire
That pierced the cloud   where I had hid my fear.
You shall go lest   they escape their doom.
You shall go.   Though I feared bitterly
When his hand   was thus upon me,
Yes, I said, here I am   LORD, sent me.

What is the fate   of the beautiful people,
Will they win in the end?   What of the siege,
How far does   the field extend?
What is not written   is told alone by age,
But the warning   is not for them,
But lands turned inland   far from sea.
Yes LORD, will you not   send me to the beautiful,
Lest the day come   and they know it not?

Such a strong   and handsome people,
Theirs is a marvelous land,   good above others,
Shall they not hear   the warning voice?
Amen and Amen,   so be it then,
There thy voice   shall dwell.
I know this peoples'   boundless beauty,
But their foreheads   are as flint.
A diamond shall   thy forehead be,

Thy words a new   sharped sword,
Lest they hear me   and restore my word,
I give thee the vision   of the land.
And he gave me   a colored glass to see with,
And a written scroll   to speak the warning word.
I opened my mouth   and ate the scroll
knew the words   that it spoke
And warning to   the people thus I took.

EMBASSY

On the road ahead
to the unbelievable event,
it's too late to wonder
how I got to be singing
a King who inspires
the young to fruition
when they are old.

Maybe it was in the sky, two hands holding gold flares,
but who had any idea what it was?
A Turner, call it an angel burning
thirty years before my waking
who knew what was seen,
Prompted by a night's dream,
realized long after seeing,
incapable of saying such a thing.

When a King comes
we lose our heads dancing,
extravagant souls
who love that appearing
of a Hero preceded a long way
by   of
embassies   delight.

TALK

When it comes to talk
everything is song,
a water breath for gills
breathes song and sings,
breathe song and sing,
they sing, they sing,
Everything has breath.
Everything that has breath.

Everything with breath connects
beneath the silent disconnect,
pure as flame that disappears
in sight and sound forget.

It comes to all who breathe
that water breath, gill song,
a temporary exhalation
that everything else that will have breath
is breathing all along.

Yourself, to meditate a roof below,
communes a creature like no other,
so unique at times at least to say
no matter what I knew that day
when everything had breath. Here I am.

Breath inspires talk,
language, expression, thought,
suddenness of wings,
a base of wind, of dust and sun,
cry of a moment, each moment timed,
three hundred eternal

breaths with the same.
Anything that's done or so recalls
is breathing the same breath as all.

That's what breath in search of talk
like any unique thing means,
Sound of breath.
Everything seeks song unconfined,
for air and water breathers' breath of gills
breathe life, breathe song and sing.

They sing.
They sing.
Everything has breath.
Everything has breath.
Everything that has breath.

NUT

Behold a thing the Lord has done
Bordered in a shell of walnuts
Hemmed in a dark kernel
Barked it all. Crack me,
The fruit I bare is thine.

NOTE

It sounds like our own lives when the editor of the Facsimile of 1910, J. Gwenogvryn Evans, says none has suffered like the text of Taliesin: "hundreds of lines have been marred in transcription. Syllables, words, clauses, sentences, lines have been dropped, prefixes, endings, and catchwords repeated or substituted for the original phrasing." Heroes are measured in epithets. No incident is completely described. Descriptions of battle are heightened with fusion from true poems, "kindled" from an oral history. Biblical and prophetic subjects, mythologies, riddles, proverbs, elegies and praises in the mead hall were all added to elements from a ninth century saga and twelve elegies of the sixth. Archaism and anachronism occur in "Song" where the association is broadened from the three hundred to the later poet Sion Eos. Verse forms that did not exist in either sixth or twelfth century Wales occur when poetic translations get the last word, from Charles Williams' Taliessin through Logres (1938) to the Matter of Britain of Tennyson's Taliessin.

The Gododdin relates (c. 580) that three hundred mounted assaulted ten thousand Anglo-Saxons on foot. Taliesin must have heard an early version or discussed the battle from echoes to the Gododdin in "On the Death of Three Hundred" and "Song." In continual reimagining he wanders among the fallen of "bright Gwynedd's horde" composing in and out of body. In "Field" the narrator elegizes the fallen by the first light of day, and after, as "long the days and long the nights I held this image in my mind of red on gold." The "flowers" and "furrows," "sweep the valley to a glade." He repeats "bright battalions with their blue bright swords," the "white lances," "steel blades by heaps of dead." "Already ravens were croaking above blood." They are all killed in the glade that "thunders one hill" and "rests its back into the ground so still." We don't know who comes "at last no more from my grave." It cannot be the narrator since the song must be finished in "bleeding to sing this song." That return at dawn the next day, when two die, gave "a second way." Who "strolled, arm and arms in the glade," one arm severed, but still carrying a sword? It suggests a surrogate, and not Aneirin either, some other whose name we don't know, the unknown soldier whose pay is to "bend and shake like the corn." Three is a poetic number. One stands for three and three for three hundred and three hundred for them all.

The sublimated garden where the "Red Head" is both annual and perennial, grows from root and seed to symbolize the late blooming that prolongs and foreshortens the life, the bloom "that died alone in the sunlit plain...that will not return alone." This is the "crimson head in the spring-brightened loam." Death "only increases their yield." "I lay on the bloody field, I it was who bled." It describes the shed blood as "barley feed" and himself a plough man "rich in cultivation," a farmer of the fallen. Survival then burial is implicit in the muscle twitching after death, "the grasses, the aired bodies, stir about the break of day." He calls them first flowers, then grasses, then flowers of purple blades.

The sonnets in praise of Jesus, rough and smooth Welsh timbers craving for the worship of God and many more mysterious poems added to the elegies such as "The Branch" might reread, "When the Lord of All descended into death." "The Plant" and "Love-Lies-Bleeding" sublimate to complete the meditation of red on gold. "The Plant," is as unknown as the soldier, who "though you know me not," "grows nearer to "where my Lord his veins let flow." That he bleeds "with him for he loves the world," repeats that "He loves the world with his own shed blood" which produces "these seeds he would sow," in the redemption of the world. "Angel Standing in the Sun," is related to The Fire of Love of Richard Rolle, where the song of angels resounds, signifying union with divine love. The editor of Penny, George Dance, suggests "on one level, it's a literal (vision of an) angel seen in the sun...on another, the last line makes me think of Southwell's vision of "The Burning Babe" - that (and the son/sun pun) get me to read it as a poem to Jesus, which works well on a Good Friday. Then there's the foreshadowing of Schwartz's poem, and its "Time is the fire in which we burn", which gets me thinking about life itself as a process of controlled burning."

The poem first appeared in A Calendar (1973) as "On Turner's Angel Standing in the Sun, 1846." Viewing the painting at the Tate Gallery after Calendar's appearance, the last words of that brilliant colorist J. M. W. Turner come to mind, "the sun is god." Unfortunately for the Sun King (le Roi Soleil) of the modern Louis VIV at his assembly in Versailles and sycophants of Apollo who construe the Jordan Lead Codices as figures of Christ, or the French president Emmanuel Macron declaring he will govern France like Jupiter, the Roman king of the gods and even the American president Donald Trump's image of Apollo in his golden penthouse, there will be no Golden Age. This epiphany the Dayesman comes to judge. Then comes the feast of the birds and the burial of Gog that takes 7 months, whose weapons provide firewood for 7 years.

Theophanies debating whether these were angels or in fact the One appearing, the likeness of the heart to fire and light and its reception in images of color and sound in the heart of man of line 2 of "Angel," renew in the next to the last line, my heart, in which brightness is all the end of life. The wings of angel's gold, beings light radiant of golden man, like appearances to Daniel, Jacob or Abraham, are the brightness and glory of the First Begotten. The Daysman of Judgement (Job 9.33) of the angel in the event that follows, which word appears in the 1551 edition of 1 Samuel 2:25 of the English Version of the Bible translated "dayes-man," in Tyndale's translation for Exodus 21:22 reads, "He shall paye as the dayesmen appoynte him" (as the "judges determine"). So hence the Son of Man is "the dayspring from on high" of Luke 1.78, titled in Peter the First Begotten. The speaker's heart is consumed in His fire, for Our God is a consuming fire. The True Light That Lights everyone who comes into the world includes John's injunction, "Wake up, O sleeper, rise up from the dead, and Christ will shine on you." He is the Only Begotten and First Begotten, "First born among many brethren" (Romans 8.29).

<u>Matthew Henry Commentary</u> says Christ has many crowns, for he is King of kings, and Lord of lords. He is arrayed in a vesture dipped in his own blood, by which he purchased his power as Mediator; and in the blood of his enemies, over whom he always prevails. His name is The Word of God; a name none fully knows but himself; only this we know, that this Word was God manifest in the flesh; but his perfections cannot be fully understood by any creature. Angels and saints follow, and are like Christ in their armor of purity and righteousness. The threatenings of the written word he is going to execute on his enemies. The ensigns of his authority are his name; asserting his authority and power, warning the most powerful princes to submit, or they must fall before him. The powers of earth and hell make their utmost effort. These verses declare important events, foretold by the prophets. These persons were not excused because they did what their leaders bade them. How vain will be the plea of many sinners at the great day! We followed our guides; we did as we saw others do! God has given a rule to walk by, in his word; neither the example of the most, nor of the chief, must influence us contrary thereto. He is the glorious Head of the church, is described as on a white horse, the emblem of justice and holiness.

As a sonnet, rhyming in triplets at that, not a venial sin, "Angel" may offend polities and pieties. The editor of Awhile, had already invited the author to repent: "If you have not truly repented, we advise you to do so, because the Master may return the next moment, and it wouldn't be so good for you to get others prepared but be left behind."

This is not to suggest that editor has knowledge of the hundred shortcomings and regrets so well established that a vow in the present to pay and repay the debt of kindness owed all living creatures always seeks to increase. I am grateful to Awhile for publishing both "Angel Standing in the Sun" and "The Plant" before others would. The editor further invites, should one more effort be admitted, "If your work is accepted up to three times you will be called into Awhile family as a Writer or an Artist." Which is not to be scorned for we do not receive many, if any, such invites.

A statement on Angel Standing in the Sun in the Turner Collection at the Tate Gallery indicates "this late painting shows the Archangel Michael appearing on the Day of Judgement with his flaming sword. In the foreground are Old Testament scenes of murder and betrayal: Adam and Eve weep over the body of Abel (left), and Judith stands over the headless body of Holofernes (right). Turner's pessimistic picture seems to show death is everywhere in this fallen world...he showed the painting with lines describing 'the feast of vultures when the day is done.' which is the biblical reference, "And I saw an angel standing in the sun; and he cried with a loud voice, saying to all the fowls that fly in the midst of heaven, Come and gather yourselves together unto the supper of the great God (KJV)." That supper is the subject of "The Banquet of God," displayed in the 20th anniversary edition of Ygdrasil, May 2013. Angel was on the cover of the first Awhile, a site out of Uyo Nigeria that was hacked pirated, repossessed, exceeded and expired. All the more reason to thank Penny.

"The Bright Extensive Will" also appeared at Penny, where sons of angel light bow from out the sky, blind in all their beams and enter creation, which resembles those in Paradise Lost with the First Begotten who "by the waters of life, where'er they sat / In fellowships of joy the sons of light hasted."In looking for alternatives to war, peace oddly is on one hand and tyranny the other. War is the happy middle ground. Arms and the man fight for autonomy there. It just depends on what side you are on.